A Sceptic's Guide

to

POLITICS

also by Peter Vaux

DM's DICTIONARY

of Alternative Management Terms

A Sceptic's Thesaurus

A Sceptic's Guide
to
POLITICS

by

Peter Vaux

Published by

DM
PRODUCTIONS

P.O.Box 218 DISS IP22 1QY United Kingdom

Copyright 2001 by Peter Vaux

The right of Peter Vaux to be identified as the author of this work has been asserted in accordance with the Copyright, Designs and Patents Act 1988.

British Library Cataloguing in Publication Data
A Catalogue record of this book is available from
The British Library

ISBN 0 9536161 1 8

All rights reserved. No part of this publication may be reproduced, stored in a retrieval system, or transmitted, in any form or by any means, electronic, mechanical, photocopying, recording or otherwise, without the prior written permission of the publishers.

This book may not be lent, resold, hired out or otherwise disposed of by way of trade in any form, binding or cover other than that in which it is published without prior consent of the publishers.

Cartoon illustrations by Dominic Miéville
Cover design and typeset by Geraldine Florio
Cover photograph by Giulia Andreotti
Set in Sabon and Frutiger Roman

Printed in Great Britain by
The St Edmundsbury Press Ltd
Bury St Edmunds, Suffolk

To truly Honourable Members

and more especially

to the rest of us

who put them there

(or don't).

Contents

Acknowledgements

I would like to thank the late SS "Peche" Harrison for his inspirational irreverence, blended with strength, kindness and generosity. My late mother Luki for her wonderful sense of humour, her deep bewilderment at the follies of the world, and of politics and politicians (not quite the same thing).

My debt to friends is extensive. In particular I would like to thank Richard Wright and David Wright for their rare gift for humour which off-sets their public roles.

I have been privileged to have had an education (for which I am particularly indebted to my father) that valued humour, almost as highly as independence and learning, though it is of course also deeply embedded in the British tradition, and this book makes no claims to any of them! The failures of current educational drift, not exclusive to the UK, will not, it is hoped, exclude these qualities from the league tables.

My debt is inevitably also to those who are engaged in politics, in whatever sphere.

Without them, there would be no satire, and very little media, which is partly based on self-recognition, if not empathy.

I am grateful to Geraldine Florio for working calmly in the face of difficulty and for her generosity and expertise. To Denis Harman, for his support at St Edmundsbury Press. Also to Giulia Andreotti for the photo, on which the front cover is based.

Once more, in the background, Pamela and Sophie have played a vital role.

Responsibility for the contents of this book remains, of course, entirely my own.

Preface

Politics and politicians seem to have reached the nadir of their popularity, at least their zenith of unpopularity, which is perhaps a good thing, at least for them. There is only one way to go.

The reasons are complex. The structure of society has changed, our knowledge of their "game" has become deeper and more sophisticated, as it has of their natures, exposed often in the crude limelight of the press.

On the one hand we want more, though, from experience, we expect less. We want our public figures to be characters of myth and yet we know them as people, warts and all. Can we have it both ways? Evidently, only if the rules and nature of the game change, as with our expectations.

Here there seems to be a huge gap between what we want (or think we want), and need, and what is deliverable in the current formats of representation and party politics. The need has gone beyond its capacity to deliver.

Yet we remain privileged to live in an evolving democracy, indeed in a democracy at all.

The fact that politics and politicians are the butt of many of our jokes, despair, amazement, does not mean that what they do (or don't do) is not serious or important.

Psychologically we need people to blame, to ridicule, to trivialise, if only, perhaps, to off-load our own failures, but also, perhaps, as some nervous recognition that the activity is important enough to be made light of.

Nevertheless, it is we who vote for the people who come to powerlessness. And retain the ability to get rid of as much as to elect Honourable Members to the Mother Of All Parliaments (soon, no doubt, to be European, eventually, God forbid, Worldwide).

This little book is, it is hoped, really an entertainment. A small contribution to a way of seeing and looking at politics and politicians. I have not yet met anyone from another country who does not have a sense of humour, though there may be one or two who do their best not to show it. We are all citizens of the world.

If there is a more serious aim it is, in a small way, to remind us constantly of the need for humour as well as vigilance in the complex muddle that democracy is. Satire prevails upon us to be vigilant when regarding those who seek or hold power. A brief look around the UK, and beyond across the international landscape, reminds us of how constant that need is.

The need for humility is always present. It does not appear to be consistent with those who seek power to have this characteristic in abundance.

In this context satire can not only bear witness, but be restorative.

The Golden age, it would seem, only applies to particular groups of people, for specific periods of time, and is never all-encompassing, except in imagination.

Even the disenfranchised - perhaps most of all those apparently growing numbers - are involved. These are not always acting out of apathy, but rather sometimes from a conscious disinterest, which can be as much an explicit political statement as might be their vote against the candidate they did not really wish to choose.

The choice of words has been largely intuitive, reflecting those which have come to me in the writing process. I am aware that it is far from exhaustive, and that I have not always got the balance right. A few have appeared in a previous book, "DM's Dictionary of Alternative Management Terms/A Sceptic's Thesaurus", (which, in view of the proliferation of management terms into politics, might be regarded as a companion book), though are perhaps more apt here.

Let us keep democracy alive! Let us continue to self-question, tease ourselves and our political masters, in case we forget that our lives are short and that we must not subject ourselves to the trivial indulgences of big egos without our approval or tacit consent even when, especially when, in the broader sphere, we cannot, or do not, agree with a decision made. Let us protect politicians from themselves, and then us!

Peter Vaux
Suffolk
June 2001

"What do you know of this business?"

"Nothing," said Alice

"Nothing ***whatever***?" persisted the King

"Nothing whatever," said Alice

"That's very important," the King said, turning to the jury. They were just beginning to write this down on their slates, when the White Rabbit interrupted: "***Un***important, your Majesty means, of course," he said in a very respectful tone, but frowning and making faces at him as he spoke.

"Unimportant, of course, I meant," the King hastily said, and went on to himself in an undertone, "important-unimportant-unimportant-important----" " as if he were trying which word sounded best.

from "Alice in Wonderland" by Lewis Carroll

A

abstain

Three people come to the door. One to sell you walking shoes; the second, slush puppies; the third, creepers.

What you really want is an overcoat.

"CREEPERS", "SLUSH PUPPIES", "WALKING SHOES"?
"NO THANKS!"

Act of Union

The integration of opposites in the act of creation.

Hence The Manchester United Kingdom, but not all other European Communities.

activist

Minority person with great, if sometimes misdirected, energy, sometimes useful in generating real change. Political activist: breezebag.

A

administration

American term meaning power, occasionally referring to the executive patronage bestowed on the random will-have-beens chosen by The President.

Elsewhere, as in the UK, may be mistaken for the Civil Service.

agenda

Printed schedule of topics for consideration at a meeting, normally ignored, certainly discussed in a different order and always including items that shouldn't be there.

Political agenda refers to personal ambitions packaged as policy intentions, neither of which are generally fulfilled. Fortunately.

adversarial

Form of politics (as in law) in which people take different or opposite views for the purposes of the debate, as opposed to with the intention of improving the substance or the nature of the discussion, and with no real interest or bearing on the outcome. Hence ideal for The UK Parliament, and better than those sober Scandinavian political processes which are so bloody boring and equally ineffective.

A

all-night sitting

Having spent the day in debate, but more likely the pub, MPs get down to their second favourite nocturnal pursuit, squabbling over the dispatch box, as part of the undue parliamentary process of advancement, while their eyes gradually close.

Sometimes an all-night vigil held in either house in which Honourabble Members fall asleep while talking (at the beginning), and the speaker (in the mi/uddle).

Alternative to all day sitting, which rarely happens, as nobody's ever there.

ALL NIGHT SITTING

A

ambassador

A rather distinguished representative of another notional government and generally invisible.

Loves canapés, and prefers not to be seen not looking, and never holds opinions, merely states alternative propositions (if pushed).

Brought to account by the host nation when there is an incident, as when a bomb falls on an embassy, or when an alleged spy plane is shot down.

Worth their weight in bullion and would be highly sought after people if it weren't for the fact that their loyalty is to their governments, something that no outsider (and not many insiders) can understand.

Though it's better than to be loyal to somebody else's-eds.

amendment

As in the 5th, 6th, 23rd....

The number of drafts it takes to make an EU document readable.

Also the number of languages into which it must be mistranslated, for the purpose of corporate unity. Thank God for English, William and St Georgiana.

A

aristocracy

People once born into the apparent privilege of a title whose ancestry fought (or bought) their way up the slippery slope and managed to stay there long enough to continue to make the right donations.

Tend to be a-political with a small c, as it takes most of them a hour to get up the stairs to the chamber anyway. Now with no assets and very little intellectual property.

Alternatively those with a finely tuned mind, who have worked through their own garbage and have come out the other side with perhaps a little bit of wisdom and certainly humility. Hence not the terrain of politicians.

audit

A form of accounting or monitoring, eg of public accounts: making sure that extravagant waste is presented as essential expenditure.

autobiography

A document in the guise of a book claiming to have been written by the named author, about whose life it claims to be the definitive account.

The threat that one might be written increases the advance substantially.

The vain hope that one might not be written brings sighs of relief from all those trees.

B

baggage

What you unavoidably bring to the party but rather you'd left in the cupboard along with your previous convictions, ex-lovers and other exhumations/skeletons.

"Intellectual baggage" means that you wrote or said certain things in the past which are wholly untenable now (and were then) so you defend them with even more vigour, in the process of not being seen to change your mind (again).

balance of power

When a third party has the same as or more seats than the difference between the seats held by the two main parties.

A form of disproportionate leverage.

ballot box

A box with a slit in the top.

To vote: Take the ballot paper. Place a cross (or squiggle) against the name of the person (never the party) least incapable of representing your views, but not his own interests, in the next Parliament (rarely beyond), or other existential retreat, and throw it in.

Alternatively you could look at the list, collapse in a fit of hysterics and go and have a half litre.

Three cheers for democracy.

ball-park

A figure of speech meaning, "roughly speaking", or "about", to describe government spending estimates on important projects, such as the Mile-endium Doom, and other fiascos, which are hopelessly conservative with a Creditor's "c" and could perhaps have been better spent elsewhere. The NHS, Schools, for instance.

beer-and-sandwiches

A phrase formerly describing the relationship between a (then, as now, rare) Labour Government and the TUC (Terribly Under-represented Comrades), especially how they conduct their business and settle their similarities - ie in secret, downing flat ale and scoffing cheese and pickle on white.

Now known as chilli con chardonnay (Tuscan).

The minutes are available should any one wish to see them.

Don't all rush at once.

Big Bong

A huge erect thing that strikes day and night to remind

Honourable Members of their priorities.

The best known landmark in the world, or Parliament Square.

Also known as Little Ben or Big Nelly.

Black Rod

The man who tries to break into the Upper Crusty House when the door's shut. Not quite the same thing as Guido.

budget

Biannual monologue delivered as if it were a speech by The Chancellor of The Red Box outlining plans for fiscal rip-offery, known as taxes by the back door, or how to screw the public as much as possible while appearing to be fair to every-one (except pensioners and the unemployed).

An important indicator of the stealth of the economy, perhaps even how far away we are from another, what are they called now....ballot box farces.

by-election

An election that occurs following the death, say (or other unfortunate event), of the sitting MP, which has no bearing at all on the mood of the country, and even less on the local electorate.

C

Cabinet Office

Pass.

campaign

The way in which a siege, or war or election is fought, involving, research, planning, resource allocation, and careful application, in which speed, conning, adaptability and belligerence are prominent. Money also helps.

In effect an ad hoc process subject to the whims of time, the weather and the electorate, as well as unredeemable chaos caused by the media, chief whips and strategists.

canteen

Apparently very good in The House of Commons, if not The Castle of Lords: plenty of Yoghurt and Vegeburgers, unlicensed (except for tea) for the politically inapt.

CAP

Can Anyone Please explain, Monsieur Le President, how this Chronically Awful Policy can continue? Cows Are Passez.

C

The Chancellor of The Exchequer

The person in charge of the purse strings, not to be confused with the Chief of The Bundesbank.

charisma

The secret personality ingredient that separates the followable from the reliable, and normally includes a pinch of the fundamentalist. Hence undesirable.

As opposed to Charm, which is not as common as you might wish, and doesn't deliver either.

Chequers

The Official Country retreat of the Prime Minister, where he goes when the going gets tough or he needs to let the dog have a bit more of a run than in St James' Park.

Also a place for discreet entertainment, of friends, media types, even dignitaries, for off-the-record non-events.

co-alition

To be in bed with the opposition for as long as it's mutually highly strung.

Commonwealth

An undervalued group of previously incompatible nation states, now bound by a common anxiety and nostalgia, providing great wealth and breadth of experience, and markets. Should be restored to its former infamy.

Communism

A belief system which makes everyone equal, in principle. True as far as God is concerned. Almost true as far as the tax person.

It also believes in holding on to the abuse of power at all costs. Not unlike some other belief systems.

community

Group of people with a sense of mutual belonging, a relatively common purpose, shared experience, and never very materially wealthy. Once the foundation of society until we were led to believe that there were only individuals.

Also a place where such people live.

Now replaced by anti-social capital.

consensus

Reaching apparent unity by common disagreement. A win, win, win scenario loved by consultants and The European Commission.

Hence the speed, coherence and effectiveness of their decisions.

C

Conservative

Someone who is nostalgic for a past which never existed but whose illusions, it is claimed, are worth fighting for, including lower taxes, a free market and flexible (cheap) labour.

A broad church that includes everything from lay people to high priests, rampant free marketeers to euro bashers, one nation to old nation tories, soon to be relabelled New Conservative, also known as Old Favours.

constituency

The place misrepresented by an Honourable Member (not to be confused with an M of P), who normally lives elsewhere.

Of variable size, constitution and political relevance. Hence most of us have never heard of our M of P's name.

constitution

The framework of government, often written down according to sound, but impracticable principles, or made up as you go along, as is the case in The UK.

constitutional/structural reform

Political equivalent of corporate culture change which promises change as opposed to improvement, and delivers neither.

cross-party

A form of political cross-dressing which means that you can swap sides, or take a bi-partisan view, which is useful for such important issues as MPs' pay.

deal

Now The New Deal. Or pick a card from the pack and take your chances.

delegate

Person who attends the annual non-events at Bournemouth, Eastbourne and Blackpool at which speeches are made and platitudes proliferate, but where innovators (trouble-makers) are kept quiet, in case anyone might want to hear.

democracy

Giving everyone a say in the way they are misrepresented, as opposed to how they are mismanaged, from which governments are formed, dissolve and re-emerge in the guise of another (even the same) party, especially if you are New Conservative, as opposed to Old Favours - after another of those ballot box farces.

Worth fighting for.

Ancient word meaning survival of the richest.

deprived area

A place in chronic need of help, money and other hand-outs from The European Umbilical Fund, often with high unemployment, crumbling services and desperately poor housing.

Occasionally visited by politicians under duress, if there's a good photo opportunity.

de-select

The political equivalent of de-bagging in honour of the fact that you'd have done it yourself a few days back with The Chairman's wife (allegedly), had the opportunity arisen.

despotism

Megalomania with gangrene.

devolution

Examples include The Scottish Parliament, The Welsh Assembly, The Northern Irish Assembly and the soon to-be-redesigned English House of Commonplaces (next to The Thames).

Part of the fragmentation of power that belies the increased drive for centralisation of the large power blocks, such as The European Parliament.

Giving power back to the people, at least to local politicians.

D

diplomacy

What some Ministers do to stave off the opposition without engaging in the tiresome business of debate.

Otherwise known as appeasement, or it's a near Knock-Out.

disenfranchised

A term describing people's sense of alienation, mainly from politics, politicians, and the political process, but probably also from life in general, which is difficult to understand for people who want attention and power at almost any cost.

Alternatively, people who couldn't give a banana skin about politics.

Anybody out there?

D

dispatch box

The place from which The Prime-Cut, Meat-Off-The-Bone Minister, also known as the leader of the former opposition, gives important massages to Parliament and the people, if they're watching the show live on digital, pay-as-you-earn, license free TV, unless you're washing socks, or would prefer to turn off.

A lectern like thing against which The PM releases his tension (& the odd idea) on the unsuspecting public by leaning forward and bashing the top hard with a clenched fist, whilst waiting intently for the "hear! hears!" of his own party and the jeers of the soon to be next Prime-Cut Minister's current dismembered leader of Her Majesty's Whatsit party opposite.

Rarely a place from which speeches are given or, more likely, read.

donor

Anything from a rich but secretive sponsor of a political party, to a giver of blood.

Which do you think's more important?

down-turn

A euphemism for economic revival misinterpreted as the chronic state of the economy.

E

EC

Choose one of the following (if necessary)

European Collaboration

European Co-operative

European Collective

Communauté Européenne

European Confederacy

European C.ntrick

economic cycle

Waves of success and negative profit, assuming there's enough wind (no question) and you can hold on.

e-democracy

Adding to the chaos, e-xponentially.

electioneering

Social equivalent of engineering.

Eleventh Commandment

Thou shalt not - what is it now? Get caught with your pants down.

Or with anybody else's.

E

euro

A currency designed to increase European integration and enhance European competitiveness, likely to increase instability and fragmentation.

Europe

A large area of the map at the western end of Asia (more properly, the eastern side of The Atlantic), comprising lots of states (once called nation states, but increasingly a federation of incompatible regions), with huge historical differences, disunited by a common culture.

Rather inward looking and is integrated against the natural geo-position of its various entities.

European Parliament

An experiment in transnational democracy based on anything from 1.5% of votes from the electorate (parts of the UK) to about 75% (Luxemburg, apparently), some of whom don't even know where it sits, which isn't surprising as it moves around.

An important experiment, otherwise known as the multinational waffle factory.

God knows what it will be like when there are 25, 26, 27, 28 members.

And then what?

The Pan World Trade mis-alliance? The Mid-Eastern Self-Protection rocket. The Far-Eastern Self-Aggrandisement project.

Or just, Humanity?

exit poll

Sampling the views of people who have just voted as a means of predicting the outcome before the party's over (in some cases, literally).

About as reliable (and readable) as party manifestos (or partly manifestotos), or indeed entry polls which is what people tell you they intend to vote before they go in as a means of confirming their membership of a focus group.

expert

A person with strong opinions, the opportunity to air them and an audience who is gullible enough to believe in them.

That rules out politicians.

Not to be confused with an authority, who really knows what he/she is talking about, whose opinions are rarely sought and even more rarely listened to.

Authorities are eminent as opposed to experts who are prominent, although some people would argue there are some exceptions who are both.

That also rules out politicians.

European Commission

The weak executive wing of the European Government in waiting.

farce

Form of light entertainment in which the Players come on stage, mouth a few platitudes, run amok whilst we all convulse, then exit left, followed by a mistress and the press. Has no bearing at all on The House of Commons.

far left

The dribbler of the left who beats the right back, but can't get the ball across as it's now on the wrong foot.

The bane of the soft left (who can end up as Commissionaires.)

far middle

The centre forward who would head the ball home, if only the wingers could stop poncing about and get the ball across.

Also known as the Fair Muddle.

far right

The dribbler of the right whose ball has gone out of play.

fiasco

Not so much banana skins as "who's nicked the uranium rods" and sold them on the cheap in Dubious-eye.

F

floating voter

Person who doesn't know which way to vote on the day, or any other day, (is sometimes carried by the wind - but not his), and remains poker-faced (ie confused) until the last minute when he decides to abstain. Not to be confused with floating abstainer who's way off base man, and not likely to come back.

focus group

Groupie or grope therapy.

F

Foreign Secretary

A vital role, often filled by a most distinguished person, Minister.

Has been described as the Foreign and I speak French tolerably well Secretary, who does a damned fine job under difficult circumstances, like slashed budgets and the other outcomes of consultants' improvement strategies, and global restructuring.

This, despite new delegations in important places such as Tajizikstan, following advice from Mr President who is, allegedly, still looking for it on the map.

free and fair

A phrase attributed to democratic elections.

freedom of speechlessness

One of the richest constituent elements in a democracy, neither to be abused, nor abandoned.

freedom of information

Radical proposition that assumes people are responsible and should know more of what's going on, like who spends their cash and where it goes to.

Alternatively you might be a politician and favour the freedom of misinformation.

F

fund-raising

The sort of thing senior law officers would never do in their capacity as supra-political people.

This is why The House of Lords is full of white-haired media people (and bishops) unable to tie up their own shoe laces.

G

GDP

Gradually Declining Path.

govern

A mixture of mislead and mismanage.

You could say it's throwing complexity to the wind and hoping it comes back in the form of policy. Or you could say it's a form of chaos.

Either way it's only the paranoid who survive.

And the rest of us who take the consequences.

governance

The values which we all believe in and that underlie government and other institutional control.

"You scratch my back and I'll give you a share option."

government

Tough, this one.

OK, a collection of people who are ambitious and wily, and often lawyers, who have become MPs, and then, by means beyond us and themselves, have been chosen by The Prime Minister (with advice from potential candidates and various lobby-gropes) to serve (meaning subserve) in The Cabinet, and hence rule - hey presto Britannia, or Eurotania.

green paper

Ecologically correct.

guidelines

Vague pointers.

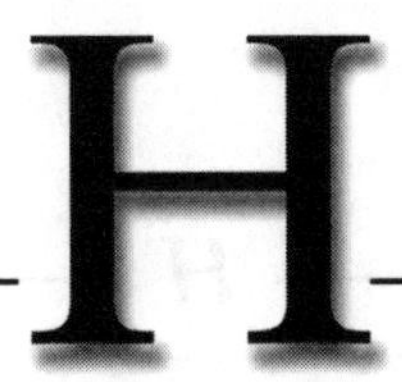

Hansard

The official record of everything that's said in Parliament which may be why it's not a best-seller.

Home Office

The Department that oversees some of what happens in England, but not Ecosseland, Wales, Northern Ireland, London and Regional Development Agencies.

Reasonabilities include: the Police, the Civil Service. That doesn't leave many left.

H

honours list

People who've served worthy causes, even businesses, possibly themselves, but not always the public, over many years, so that they may be recognised and have honour bestowed upon them (by other worthies), on earth as well as the other place, which is oddly similar to party headquarters.

HONOURS LIST

NO WONDER I CAN'T WAKE UP IN THE MORNING

Still, better than some hereditories.

H

House of Commons

A place where Honourabble people shout at each other about issues of national significance, on TV.

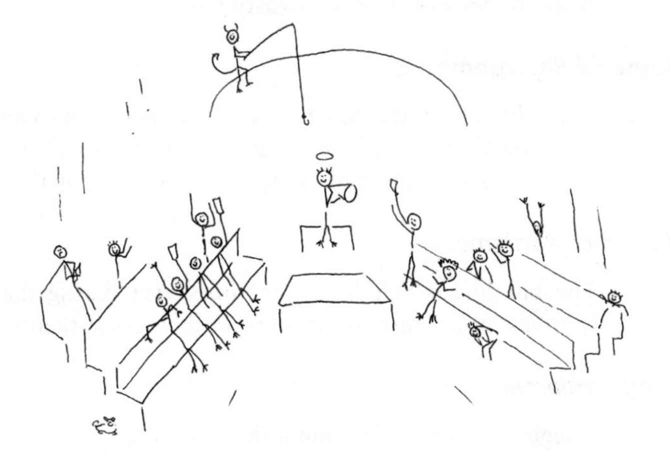

House of Lords

A red-seated Chamber full of distinguished people, some of whom have become Lords and Ladies in recognition of their achievements in Life as opposed to they will be forgotten in Death.

Formerly a retreat for the disenfranchised aristocracy, now a retreat for newly partially unelected and uplifted party political sponsors.

Also known as the Upper-Crusty House.

House of Representatives

You'd better ask the Americans. We'd prefer not to comment, until the US edition is out (eds). Refer also to Congress and other numinous institutions across from Macdonalds.

Houses of Parliament

The building which MPs sometimes visit during the day to keep out of the rain, or away from their constituents.

hung parliament

Caught between a fool and a dumb space.

I

idealist

Someone who goes into politics to make society a better place.

interview

There now follows a partly political broadcast

Breakfast with Toast

(or The Mad Hatter's Continental)

I

Sir Toast

There is a perception, Lord of The Isles - I mean Isle...rather England, or bits of it (remember The Sceptred Isle - what happened?) that Politicians are failing to deliver? I wonder if you would comment? *(doffs his socks).*

Prime Minister

No! Humbug. Rubbish. Of course, we're no, I mean, not failing to deliver. Well, the opposition may be (I remember it well) but where are they anyway? *(laughs). (pause).* I say this toast is good. *(Peers into the realm).*

Enter servant dressed as PPS (Please Pass the [Euro] Sausages). Pours coffee into coffee cup. PM smiles, a Tuscan smile, dreaming of the collapsing opposition/a third term (already).

Toast

Have some more....*(GLARE from the producer)*...I mean....what do you mean no!.... No? How can you not comment? What makes you feel able not to give a clear unequivocal commitment, answer even? The people, rather England, expects (as do a few in Wales, Northern Island, Scotland, The City, the rest of the EC, though to a lesser degree) that politicians should be subject to those unredeemable performance measures, like the rest of the Civil Service.

PM

Well, err....I can't accept that. We have put measures, sorry, not exactly measures, in place (so our hocus pocus groups tell us) from, for example, as I said in my speech last week (or was it last year?), from providers to deliverers so that value for MPs can be best minotaured for the people, that is, you and them, I mean wee.

Toast

Codsbollocks.

PM

What?

Toast

It was two years ago.

PM

What's in 103 weeks? It's all the same. Here today, gone tomorrow. Like those cows. Burnt to a steak. *(remembering to look at the script/autocue/Alistair Fairweather-in the wings)* We've spent more on advertising in the last two years than the rest of the Millennium Doomed together. What? And you know as well as I do John. It is John, isn't it?

Toast

Frank.

PM

Frank! I'll be Glad! You know as well as I do Hank, that advertising produces profits, I means results, for the advertising industry and we in Britain, are world leaders in this field. Doesn't that tell us something? (thinks - and what else?)

Toast

But you can't run an economy on advertising? It's all illusions? What about Fishing? Manufacture? Dress-making?

PM

Precisely. I'm glad you agree. We've managed it - the economy that is - for years. (pause while he drinks coffee). Looks at his watch.

I have to go. I'm late for my design consultant.

Toast

I'm sure The Chancellor won't mind. He and Fairweather are in the same trade.

PM

(to himself) How else do you think we stay in power, John?

Smiles. Adjusts his security underwear and makes for the door.

CLOSE SHOT:
PEOPLE STARE IN AMAZEMENT

BREAKFAST WITH TOAST

I

incomes policy

Taxes by the front door.

independent inquiry

An in-depth investigation aiming to get at the truth as long as it fits in with government requirements.

index-linked

Ensuring that MPs' pensions and other consumer protection rights keep in line with inflation, or cause it.

inflation

The rate that prices increase without the equivalent increase in production/productivity.

initiative

"Spin" for an idea, packaged as a proposal. Delivered as a failed experiment.

inter-governmental conference

Somewhere between The UN and A Council of Ministers, but needing a larger supply of fuzzy Ministerial wafers. Sorry, fizzy mineral water.

I

international dialogue

Talking to each other over long distances, with no result in view or intended. A form of diplomacy enacted between important bodies such as governments and global companies, in the constant quest for strategic positioning which precedes attempted or implicit domination. Very important as people stay up all night doing it and it is better than fighting.

issues

Those things that are most important, but which are not discussed, even in private.

Labour Party

Once a nineteenth/twentieth century British tribe with understandably entrenched views, now a twenty-something century Multicultural tribe with dis-entrenched views and solid working classless lack of commitments, but committed to anything and everything, especially survival.

Otherwise known as reverse conservatism.

Also known as Old Favours.

law and order

Synonymous with law and disorder, as the gap between rich and poor widens, though there's no connection between social/ economic factors and crime - obviously not. How could we be so naive?

land of nod

An imaginary place, where anything can happen, but rarely does, visited by Honourable Members while attempting to listen to other Honourable Members who wish they could be there too, and will be shortly, if they go on giving this crap-awful speech, for which I stayed up so bloody late last night, in lieu of making love to the wife/husband.

landmark decision

Common sense outcome, long overdue.

L

Leader/Speaker

The MD (Megaphone Deliverer) of The House of Commonplaces. Normally given to a fair-minded person who commands the respect of the whole house (you may prefer floor, chamber, or gaming club), has strength, charisma and humility. This doesn't allow for many applicants or nominees.

Occasionally tries to control and manage the chaotic activities of the chamber by shouting "order, order" from time to time to time (should be "order, disorder"), and waiting for a reply in the form of a pause so that he can get his euro worth in. Has been known to send a Member out of the Chamber for unparliamentary behaviour.

Is that why it's so often empty?

Is a fount of procedural wisdom and normally ends up with a knighthood, which, despite what you may think, is quite compatible with unbiased service.

To the news of his elevation to a Lordship one distinguished retiring ring leader/bath chair-person is reported to have replied , "I'm still the same shape in the bath".

Unfortunately.

Good man.

L

leadership

Has been described as "paying lip service to the idea of involving people as a means of getting your own way", which is unfair and cannot apply to politics which is about consensus decision making based on a bottom-up approach (how true), focus groups, and a sharp knife (as the whips will confirm).

Hence the "wide-ranging and complex mix of principle, motivation, morality and action" (the fuller definition), does not apply in politics either, as The Thane of Cawdor knew so well, even if it's always better to get others to do the hanky panky.

leadership contests

The idea is that most HMs would not wish to become PM, should the opportunity arise, as they haven't gone into politics for reasons of power.

Evidently not.

Tend to occur at times of crisis (like just after an election), rather than as prepared succession planning, which is no different from most disorganisations, as recent events at The BBC and BT have shown.

level playing field

If the snooker table is tilted one way it gives an advantage to the opposition, whereas if it's tilted the other way, it gives an advantage to The US (for a change).

L

Like Preferential Trade Agreements.

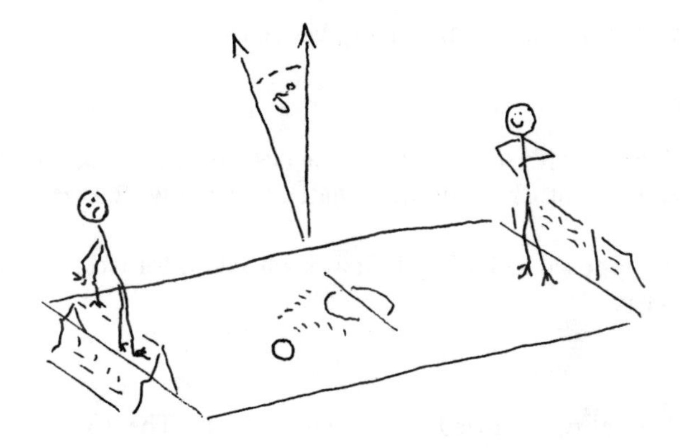

Liberal

An ancient, worthy mindlessness which tends to take an inclusive view or the muddle way along with a proportionate number of votes.

Formerly contained an admiribbald radical wing.

Liberal Democrat

One part, former breakaway group from Old Favours, who were struggling with democracy at the time (and still are), other part, Liberal.

Most people would probably wish to vote for them if they thought there was a chance of them winning something, in which unlikely event, it might be wiser not to.

L

little European

Contemporary term for Big UK man.

lobbyist

Person or persons who claim access to or influence over politicians or other group on behalf of clients with axes to grind.

As opposed to Hobby Horsists who do it for free, or MPs who get paid.

loyalty

A quality regarded as fundamental to The Knights of The Round Table, but not so evident in modern politics, as Former Prime Ministers appear to have recognised.

M

make-over wellies

Not the renaissance schemer of Italian politics but what Neuer Labour supporters wear in the countryside.

mandarin

Senior Civilian Savant, above politics, apparently, despite recent concerns, or bias, or indeed any views at all, but with a fine sense of what's best for the country, and the future of the Civil Service.

mandate

What you have been given, by the electorate, to do, but don't.

manifestoto

A slim volume, produced by each party, outlining key policies, intentions and commitments, (or committed policy intentions), in the unlikely event that they should come to power. In other words, unrealistic.

Used as a guide for voters and other impulse buyers as bedtime reading after the voting stations have closed.

In fact a rag-bag of contradictory statements brought together under the guise of a coherent set of compatible aims and objectives packaged in user-friendly form, which means alterable at a moment's notice, and not therefore to be taken too seriously.

About as reliable as company annual reports.

marginal

At the edge of, of uncertain status. No, not MPs, but the places they represent, whose allegiance is wavering, ambiguous or unclear (remind you of anybody?), and for which a special effort has to be made to win them over at times like elections.

This is when the "big guns" are brought in and swing the vote the other way.

market forces

The hidden energy that drives economic activity, capable of overwhelming power, creative and destructive, unless you live in The EU, where it is replaced by Common Market Forces, which are counterproductive to free trade and highly defensive, and are quite unaffected by global recessionary trends.

You have got to be joking.

But would you rather live in The States?

I love you America.

media

The life-blood of the egocentric and unstable who seek attention and power by almost any means. Hence all the interviews from Parliament Square.

To be treated with due care and attention, as drama and fiction are also the life-blood of the rest of humanity who are only interested in the truth in so far as it reveals something about the illusion. Hence the power of myth and Hollywood.

But not Politics.

men

Why are there so many of them in politics? See women.

MEP

An elevated form of politician, normally elected by at least 10% of constituents, neither of whom knew they existed, who's lifted above himself, not by sitting astride a horse, but by being transplanted to the obscure Parliaments of the European Economic Community, (hence with a great view of the bigger picture and therefore even more incapable of doing anything), once called the European Union, now known as pan-European Democratic Immunity.

Still, unquestionably important experiment in political activity, though improvement ideas are always welcome. Answers in cyberspace please. Winners will be drawn from a hat at the time of the next European Election, which could be any time now or then, as far as anybody knows.

Or cares.

What alternative is there?

M

Member of Parliament

Person ready to serve people at almost any cost to stay in power.

Person elected by a minority of constituents, in line with demographic principles of misrepresentation.

Person who seeks to change others in direct proportion to his inability to change himself.

Also known as Misplaced Person.

mid-term

Half way through. Life, the universe, Parliament.

Minister of State

MP in charge of a Government Department, who therefore sits in The Cabinet, and is regularly quoted because of his /her position. Occasionally gives real speeches and passes the buck in times of crisis, as part of the new interdepartmentalism of the seamless (invisible) statelessness in which we now exist. Hence the interdepartmental as opposed to regional chaos, (and the refusal of anyone to go until pushed).

Very Important Man or Woman, VIM, VIW. Paid a bit more than an ordinary fellow MP.

Works increasingly with other Ministers to give the

impression of unity as opposed to Fiefdomism.

Hires an image consultant from time to time because, it is said, "how" they appear is more important than what they say, or, certainly, think.

Useful attributes. Alleged insensitivity. Possible megalomania. Certain workaholism - ie can't keep out of the limelight in case the initiative is lost. Often clever, like the already-mentioned Italian, Mind-Over-Wellies.

minority government

Running the whole show on less than half the seats, until others can be persuaded to join or be bought into the party.

minutes

Doctored notes purporting to be verbatim, and edited for the sake of consumer clarity. Absolutely twoo. Part of open-house government and therefore not to be taken too seriously.

mission statement

Soon to be an Admission Statement, as represented by your lawyer.

multilateral

Getting governments to agree to the same statement, until it comes to the crunch or their interests are involved. Hence a contradiction in terminology.

national debt

Soon to be re-titled notional debit. Or international doubt.

national government

see also Government of National Disunity.

As opposed to notional opposition, which is what we've got at the moment.

National Lottery

Otherwise known as a general election, with even less possibility of the punter winning.

NATO

Not Another Transatlantic Ooh-lah-lah.

new economy

The unforeseeable economic future sometimes mistaken for the unforeseeable present, which is why bubbles inflate and then burst, leaving nothing but a bit of plastic on the floor.

Better to invest in the past, so as not to misunderstand where the old economy came from and could not be going.

New (pronounced Neuer) Labour

Not so much the Emperor's new clothes as his spare pair of Old Pyjamas/Favours.

Alternatively a designer label form of conservatism with a small l, aimed at the rich and famously so.

nepotism

The New School Tie.

Jobs for the persons.

night of the long knives, forks, and greasy spoons.

On le menu tonight:

bangers and mash

sausage, egg et chips

or saucissons aux boeuf provençal avec oeuf et pommes frittes

or

Sod this, bring back pounds, shillings and six pennyworth.

Payment in euros, salt free.

N

Number Ten Downing Street

A tiny little hideaway behind Whitewash Hall, where senior people come and have their photos taken, whilst shaking the hand of The Prime Minister.

Not quite the same as feeding the pigeons in Trafalgar Square, which is no longer possible.

Whose silly idea was that?

off-the-record

Comment/information given in confidence by person with the appearance of power, influence or secret knowledge to another person with all of these things and access to a wider audience and meaning, "I'm desperate to get on the telly".

on-the-record

Completely untrue.

opposition

Government in the making, or in the unravelling.

opt-out

Can I join the club, but not belong?

Oxford Union

The renowned society and debating chamber of the ancient university used as a spawning ground by clever, if articulate, debaters, some of whom later become Prominent Ministers, even lawyers, if not antique dealers.

Political equivalent of drama school. Therefore hugely enjoyable and a necessary condition for understanding Shakespeare, in the round, now known as in the inclusive.

P

package

Terms granted to senior executive to sustain life beyond redundancy.

May include share options, index-linked pension, severance pay and future advances for the auto-erotico-biography. Plus a few Euros, in case of emergencies.

Alternatively, a range of benefits given to sections of the electorate as a pay back for being members of focus groups, and other unselect committees, who misinform policy.

parliamentary correspondent

Imagine Charles Dickens, "the inimitable", sitting there, as a young writer, spell-bound in amazement and irreverence, taking notes, plotting, and imaging forth, in an ever spiralling genius of invention.

Like Honourable Members themselves, who thrive on invention, but who do not have the genius.

parliamentary procedure

The rules that keep the wheels of Parliament in motion, or not, depending on your point of no return.

parliamentary question time

A formal occasion in which pre-prepared questions are submitted to The Prime Minister, in the half-expectation of possible answers.

God knows what it would be like if it was improvised.

pendulum theory of politics, the

The idea is that you swing from left to right with a dip in the muddle, with absolute certainty, as long as the string doesn't break, or you go off the dip end.

politics

The science of manipulating public opinion in indirect proportion to misjudging it.

A triumph of the short-term over the inconsequential.

The art of survival, leading inexorably to the complicity of oblivion.

political culture

Basically, whether or not you believe in democracy.

political party

Group of people gathered together in Thy Name, labouring (so to speak) without asking for any reward save that of knowing that we do thy will, Prime Minister.

P

politically correct

Minority opinion which becomes majority assertion sometimes against the better intuitive judgement of the collective.

Term of abuse between consenting adults.

postal ballot

The opportunity to send your untampered with ballot paper by Royal Consignia.

No proof of identity necessary.

Order as many copies as you like, under as many names as you can invent, to the same or any address as no evidence of residence required.

The likelihood is that if you're not around to vote, you probably left the country for good reasons anyway.

Has anyone carried the can for this fiasco?

PPS

Pissed as a Perfumed Sausage.

PR

The art of creating and sustaining illusions.

Persuasive as RasPutin.

P

President

The Cheer Leader of American Politics, once described as the most powerful man in the world (with that button who's to argue?), now recognised as the partner of the most powerful woman.

pressure group

Collection of minor activists committed to making a single issue into one of greater importance than it sometimes deserves. **www.pressure.co.uk**

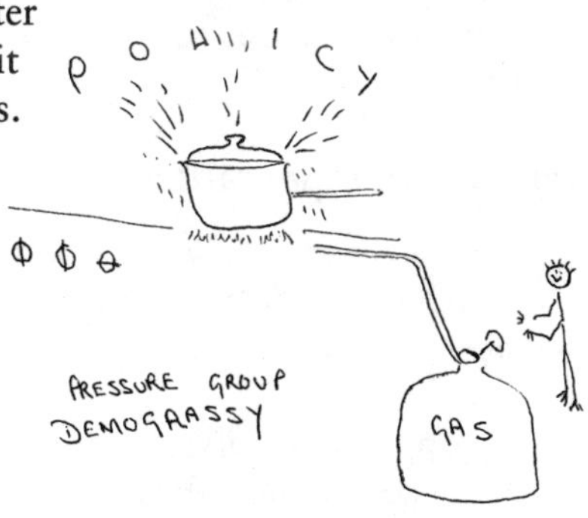

Prime Minister

The man or woman who presides over Cabinet meetings, and who led the opposition into power, now ruled by sound-bites, permanent secretaries, and impermanent officials, but whose main purpose is to stay there, and perhaps do a little good along the way to his/her place in history, with a small H, unless you are one of the very few truly great whose moment arrives in synchrony with true national, sometimes international need, paralleled by personal capability and focus.

P

privatisation

Restructuring public service entities by giving management share options and sacking staff in the process of making them less efficient.

Normally leading to increased complexity, loss of morale, and chaos, as on the railways.

Subject to The Pendulum Theory of Politics, and the inevitable return to the equivalent incompetences of public service cabals.

proportional representation

A voting system which forms a closer relationship between the number of people who vote for a party and the proportion of seats it gains.

As opposed to disproportionate misrepresentation which is what we've got at the moment.

Not that it makes much difference.

qualified majority voting

System of voting by dismembered states of The European Union which ensures that some issues can be ratified by only a majority of (powerful) former nations states, on behalf of the entire workforce, so as to make decisions quicker and statutes less effective.

As opposed to unqualified majority voting which is how most democracies creep along, unburthened towards survival, which some Honourabble Members do all the time.

No wonder The Irish rejected The Treat(y) in Nice.

quango

Quasi-autonomous non-governmental organisation, like the Civil Service. Soon to be subsumed into Regional Assembly Points (RAPs), for use to count heads in times of emergency.

Mixture between an Orang-Outang and a tango.

Or I rang, you bang and a fandango.

Queen, Her Majesty The

The Person who delivers but who doesn't write The Queen's Speech - though who would probably make a better job of it if she did.

Q

Queen's Speech

The thing that Her Majesty reads out at The Opening of Parliament in the guise of Her Majesty's Government's (you must be joking) commitments and plans for the coming season.

Judging by the way she holds her glasses you'd think she'd rather be at the races.

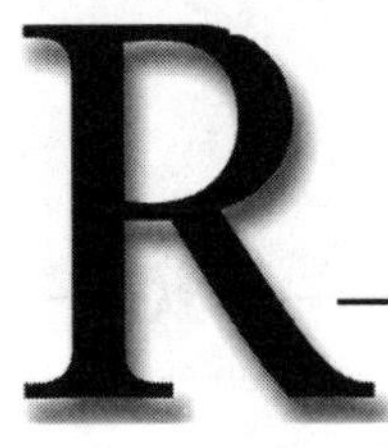

Rapid Reaction Force

A highly trained fighting force of The European Union army (also known as the Homeless Guard), ready to go into action at a moment's notice to flash points anywhere in the world, and stay there for as long as it takes to add to the chaos.

And then what?

Could start with the European Commission except that there are too many de-commissioners.

Command structure, unity of purpose, agreed methodology, guaranteed by The Italians, who don't only make good pasta, pizza and clothes, but lack the spirits of football hooliganism, apparently.

If there isn't the co-ordination and hardware to do the trick, we can always bring in the Yanks, again.

Not so much Dad's army as UN(H)C(R)'s infantry.

Soon to be re-titled the Erratic Reaction Force (ERF), according the principles of thermal underwear.

No real threat to NATO. Whatever the French might hope. Smile Mr President.

R

real politik

A phrase which describes the reality of a political situation-what can be done-as oppose to "unreal politic", which is the norm.

Also a phrase which suggests that the rest of politics is "false". Curious.

recovery

A rainbow view of the economy.

As opposed to decline which doesn't apply to The West in general or The EU in particular.

red carpet

Laid out for dignitories when they arrive at places of importance, even deep symbolic power, like airports, hotels and The House of Commons.

Something you roll out, like policy deployment, or pastry.

red tape

Something all governments try to eradicate, in the search for efficiency and improvement, especially as far as Business is concerned.

Without it of course there'd be no need for Civil Servants.

R

Also known as over-your-heads.

referendum

The ultimate democratic tool which gives voters a chance to express their views on specific issues, like who to put in power, or whether to join the Euro, or The Woro (the newly formed World Currency).

Hence not to be indulged too often, as in Switzerland.

register of interests

A place, some people call it a book, where Honourable Members write down, not the first thing that comes into their heads - we know what that is - but the first thing that goes into their bank accounts, such as consultancy fees, free trips abroad, fact-finding admissions and sponsorship walks, talks and thoughts.

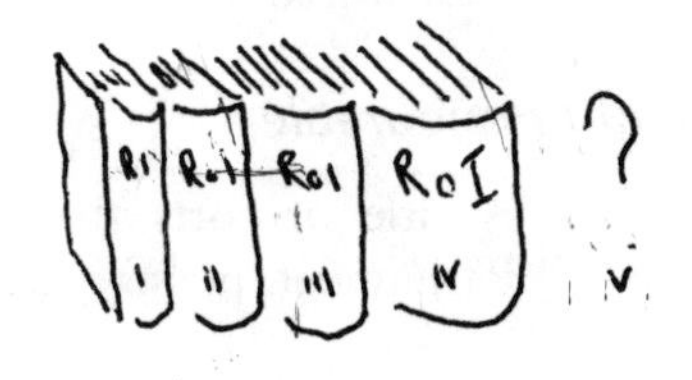

Registers of Interests, vols 1-4

This may imply that they don't devote enough time to Parliament, but it makes them people of the world.

Indeed it does.

In principle, larger than the OE(not C)D, if more provocative. In practice, thinner than partly manifestotos, and more illuminating.

Soon to be re-titled Register Of Disinterests (ROD = Return on Disinterests) which tells us in which pies there are no Honourable fingers and will make this guide look like the OED.

research

Put up your hands, count the numbers, and hey presto we have a trend.

Right Honourable

A title of sorts that is applied to a Member of the UK Parliament, possibly as compensation for lack of power.

Can't think where else this phrase would come from.

Imagine a Member of The Senate, The Reichstad or The Duma being called an Honourable Member.

The Right Honourable Member for Pennsylvania South; The Right Honourable Member for Nuremberg East; The Right Honourable Member for Vladivostok North.

How about The Diet? One suspects not, as it were.

Nod yet, anyway.

roll out

A form of policy deployment as in management, which pretends to be bottom-up, but tends to be top-down, or bottom-spread.

S

safety-net

The framework of support available to the genuinely needy, not always best served it seems by uncontrolled market capitalism, and the greatest challenge to our future prosperity.

seamless (Government)

A consultant's term meaning cross-functional or interdepartmental so that you cannot find the "seam" or the person responsible for anything.

Now widely used and increasingly invisible.

S

Secretary of State for Emulation and Enjoyment

Now known as Secretary of State for E....t.on and Who Pays The Bills.

scrutinise

To examine carefully, paying attention to detail.

Not an overt part of a politician's armoury.

security services

Fictitious organisations like MI5 and MI6 (or the M25 on a Friday evening), concerned with preserving the security of the State from internal or external threats, but not often enough (apparently) from politicians, who were after all elected on a mandate which seems to have changed since they won power.

Reputed to occupy that ghastly block South of The Thames - no, not Southwark Hospital - but actually live on park benches anywhere between Groin Park and Unconstitutional Hill. Rarely as far in the field as Bangkok or Carry-On Up The Kyber.

Occasionally infiltrated by outside agents, who seem to thrive on misinformation and double dealing.

Ring any bells?

Alternatively who sell their assets to the highest foreign

bidder, not unlike the utilities.

Known in the US as Credible Intelligence Alternative.

Sadly lacking mystery and in need of a major facelessnesslift.

Also known as insecurity services, or paranoid people. Let's hope somebody knows what they're doing.

select committee

A cross-party group of Honourable Members who do the serious work of Parliament, like scrutinising things in some detail as opposed to giving sound-bite opinions, often from a cross-party point of view. Could be a principle applied more widely but unlikely to take hold as it often requires more time away from the mistress, and might be in danger of working.

short-sharp-shock

Not, as you have been led to believe, the answer to young offenders in for a bit of military discipline, but a new form of speech making which requires Honourable Members to stick to the point, answer the questions and speak with clarity and precision.

Hence the shock.

silly season

The long summer break when there is no news, everybody is

soaking up the sun in Tuscany and enjoying other features of ordinary family life, and refreshing themselves in places that the insensible season cannot possibly reach.

social capitalism

The true wealth of communities.

spin doctor

Person who manages communication, the truth and all our perceptions, by putting the best gloss on bad news, and the most outrageous claims on the appalling.

Nobody believes it which is why they think it works.

statesmanship

Rare.

sterling

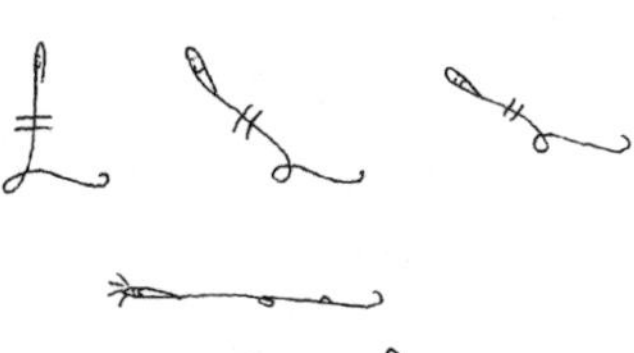

Currency needed, it is claimed, to maintain the status quo, but likely to lead to its demise.

S

summer recess

The only period when anything of value gets done and we can get back to reading novels or watching cricket.

Compare with Spring, Autumn and Winter, when Members are hard at it.

surgery

Regular event held by Member in his constituency for constituents to moan, off-load, or attempt to leverage, so as to get their axes ground. Not unlike Parliament itself.

T

tactical voting

Mis-casting for the short-term, as opposed to strategic abstention.

tantrum

What most of us, except adolescents, have inwardly, if we can't get our own way.

tax cuts

Finding other ways of screwing the public.

U

unity

The hidden bond that unites us all except political parties.

u-turn

Driving down the motorway at high speed is not the time to be doing a three point turn against the on-coming traffic, in the wind and rain, with the police up your rear.

Politicians will, occasionally, do it, for reason quite beyond us-eds.

V

vested interest

A term of endowment between consenting politicians, describing the correlation between their voting behaviour and what's in it for them. See also Register of Interests.

veto

The power to prevent a proposal from becoming European law, which isn't very common as it requires a decision to have been made in the first place.

Given to former Nation States (like The UK) to prevent Federal States from wielding too much influence, or too many vetoes.

voter

Person who elects an Honourable Member. Normally a man or a woman.

The only element in the political process (process?) who really matters. The only element in the process that is consistently ignored.

watchdog

A conscience for the powerful. Theoretically.

week

If it's long time in politics, think what it's like for the rest of us.

Westminster, Palace of

What William Wordsworth would not have written about had he been standing on Westminster Bridge a bit later.

Chief Whip

The mind boggles.

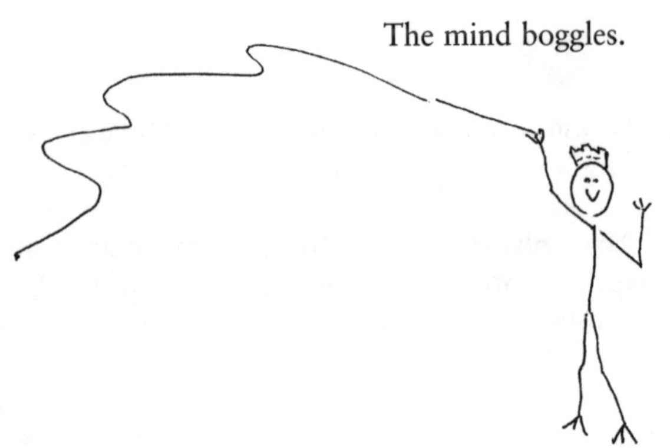

white paper

A preliminary report outlining a key policy for debate in The House of Commons, before going on to The Chamber of Ladies and returning for ratification before it becomes law.

Otherwise known as "White Rabbit" paper, as it falls down holes and has no sense of time.

wide-ranging

As in "wide ranging report...."

A report's remit or terms of reference allowing as much ground as possible to be covered in order not to come to any conclusions that could threaten action, or which might upset the apple (French) cart or the European gravy train. A means of diluting blame so that nobody takes responsibility for anything, especially the report itself.

women

Why aren't there more in politics? Need you ask.

world parliament

The inevitable outcome of the continued expansion of The EU, soon to be retitled World Community (no longer EC).

X

xenophobia

A term meaning dislike of foreigners and bandied about in times of crisis, which is curious really as most of us come from somewhere else, and will certainly be going there in due course.

Y

Yo, Minister

Should we have a more sensible policy on soft drugs?

The answer from Lambeth.

Z

zero Option

Endgame. As when it's time to have gone.

A former Old Favour's Minister is reported to have laboured too long before leaving, after his sell (your flate) by date.

zero tolerance

Talking tough on crime or any hint of criticism of their next pay rise.

Application Form
Membership of House of Lords

1. Real name:

2. Current title (delete as preferred):
   Ms/Miss/Mrs/Dr/Professor/Reverend/Mr/Master/Mischief/Other
   Member of the Lower House/Chamber/Other (e.g. Senate)

3. Preferred title (in order of preference):
   Lord/Lady/Duke/Prime Minister/Long-life UHT or Stales Very Quickly/Life Peer/Other/Umpire/Medium, right-leg over (the wicket)

4. Position sought (if different from above):
   How different?
   Are you applying to become The Queen?
   If not, is it The Presenter of Channel 4 News?
   Other?
   (For God's sake tell us)

5. Cheque enclosed (the more the better [your chances]). We recommend not less than $10, £2, or 700 Euros.
   Preferred support outlet (tick in order of priority):
   Restoration of:
   a. The aristocracy
   b. Democracy
   c. MPs' Index-linked Pensions

6. Credit Card Details:

7. Address:
   Town
   County
   Bahamas

8. Marital Status: M S D (Other)

9. Name of Mistress/lover:
   (if different from wife/husband)

10. Other defendants:

11. Are you a Member of the House of Come-ons?
    If so, which sort?

12. Do you speak English? (no preference given)
yes/no

13. Was your father born in this country? If so, tick as appropriate:
Wales
Scotland
England
London
Northern Ireland
Cornwall
(The) South West (Country, other than Cornwall)
Eastern or a bit more than East Anglia
Westminster
Yorkshire and the Humber
South East
East Midlands
West Midlands
North East
North West

Other?
Please specify:
Anywhere else?

14. Was your father born at all? (by Caesarian or other)

15. Have you ever been convicted of -
Verbal Misuse (more than once)
Experience
Integrity

16. Do you intend to give a maiden speech?
If so, is the Subject interesting?

17. Have you ever given a speech that anyone can understand?
That is less than three hours long?

18. Do you intend to give a speech at all?
(think very carefully over this one, it might swing it)

19. What have you been doing for the last 1 - 5 - 10 - 30 years?
(Answer in no less than 20 words)

20. What did you do last night?

21. What would you have done last night (if you had been given the choice)?

22. Are you one of the following? If so, which?
An Ex-Minister
Soon to be an ex-Minister
A Lawyer
An Archbishop
The Prime Minister
A mole catcher

23. Expected salary/expenses:

24. Clubs:

25. Interests
(Unregistered)

26. Do you prefer Earl Grey or Breakfast Tea?

27. Are you an expert in something (anything - other than in self-promotion)?

28. Where do you expect to be in five years' time (honestly)?

29. Five minutes' time?

Thank you for your attention

Signature (in your own handwriting, and not in pencil):

Date:

All applications will be taken seriously and considered.
The decision of The Chairperson or woman and his or her committee will be final, subject to a damned good lunch at the Savoir-Faire Grill.

Please supply your application in duplicate x thirty
First Class stamp optional
No receipt unless requested
Decision will be taken within the next thirty years
Good luck
Yours ever

Chair, Select Committee for the Future of Democracy

"*an angler in the lake of darkness*"
Shakespeare

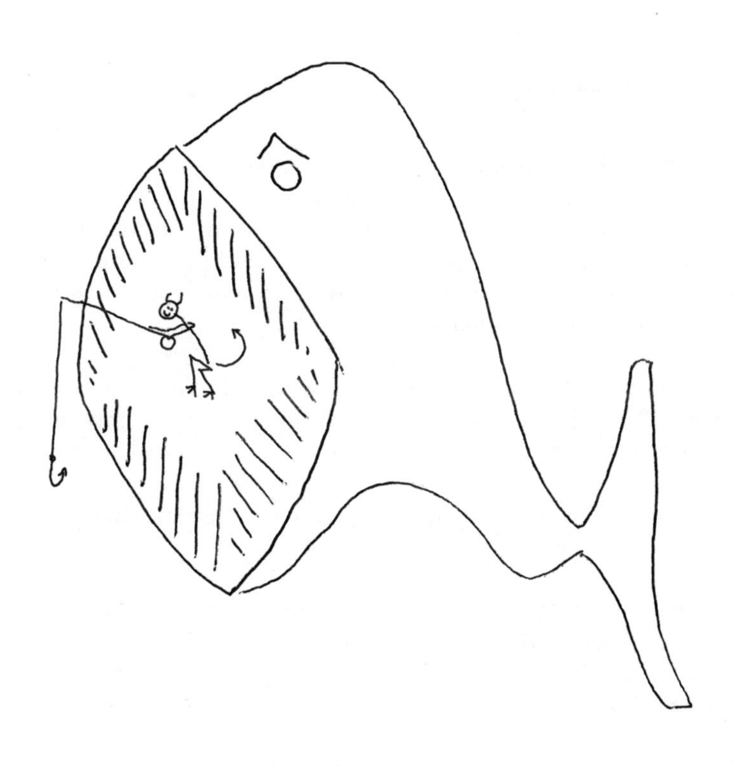

About the author

Peter Vaux is a management consultant and a writer.

As a consultant he specialises in what is known in the industry as change management, improvement strategies and culture change, all of which basically means how to make things better than they are now. Just like a politician.

He read English at Oxford as a first degree, did research in Zoology, then a PGCE. He taught for several years in London before setting up his own consultancy.

He also has his own business with various interests from publishing to film development.

His book, "DM's Dictionary of Alternative Management Terms/A Sceptic's Thesaurus", was published in 1999.

He has also written a novel, short stories, and screenplays.

Born in New York, he now lives in Suffolk, England.

Praise for

DM'S DICTIONARY
of Alternative Management Terms
A Sceptic's Thesaurus

(ISBN 0 9536161 0 X)

"I have enjoyed dipping into it"
Gerry Robinson, former chairman, The Granada group, UK

"....this dictionary will strike a chord with many....the best business people will see the humour in these definitions."
Roger Trapp, The Independent

"Perceptive....entertaining and clever....dissembling of business management jargon is expertly done."
In Touch, the magazine of The Netherlands British Chamber of Commerce

"I laughed a lot."
James Cutt, Professor of Public Administration, The University of Victoria, Canada

"A devastating blend of satire and common sense."
Peter Acton, former Vice-President, The Boston Consulting Group

"Should be compulsory reading for all civil servants."
Operations Director, supplier to UK Government

"Excruciatingly accurate!"
Jo Howard, Business Planning Director, WHSmiths, UK

"A wonderful handbook for foreigners working in The UK. It demystifies jargon and makes communication easier-and it does it with wit and style."
Pia Helena Ormerod, Senior Partner Fast Forward Communications

"Masterly."
Dena Michelli, former Business Development Director for Executive Education, The London Business School

Quoted on BBC Radio 4, BBC World Service;
featured on Bloomberg TV, Sky News